THE GROWTH OF A SHADOW

The Growth of a
S H A D O W
Selected Poems of Taejoon Moon

Translated from the Korean
WON-CHUNG KIM & CHRISTOPHER MERRILL

This is an **Autumn Hill Books** book.

Published by Autumn Hill Books, Inc.
P.O. Box 22
Iowa City, IA 52244

The publication of this book was generously supported by the Korean Literature Translation Institute.

Cover design and layout by Justin Angeles

ISBN-13: 978-0-9827466-3-9
Library of Congress Control Number: 2011943451

AB

http://www.autumnhillbooks.org

CONTENTS

part four

COLOPHON

This book was prepared using the Adobe Design Premium Creative Suite 3. Layout was done in InDesign. It has been printed by Edwards Brothers Inc. The text of this book was typeset in Goudy Old Style at 9.9/11.4.

PREFACE

Horizons, literal and imagined, inform the work of Taejoon Moon, who is regarded as one of Korea's most important younger poets. And it is said that he opened new horizons in the lyric tradition of his country, discovering in ordinary objects and situations innovative means of apprehending the world in its glorious complexity. His poems are rich in the sort of small details—the aroma of cooked rice, a butter clam emerging from its shell, a wheelbarrow in a bamboo grove—that open onto larger vistas. His attentiveness (shaped by Buddhist practice), his lively wit, his learning—these help him to see farther than most.

Thus in a defining poem like "Horizontality" a simple event becomes an occasion for a meditation on transience:

> A dragonfly alights before me,
> looks into my eyes with its beady eyes,
> spreads its transparent wings horizontally.
> Like lotus leaves, it unfurls its linen wings horizontally.
> It looks like duckweed floating on water,
> it doesn't sway to either side.
> But I turn my neck of thoughts right and left,
> and see the hole heaved up by a grub on a windy day,
> and trace the rough hands of weeds encroaching on the yard.
> Even as my thoughts sway and look to my right and left
> the dragonfly maintains its tranquil horizontality.
> Before this horizontality, the dragonfly lets
> the folding screens I raised to my right and left collapse.
> Heaven raises a terrible horizontality.

What begins in observation ends in dream and revelation; in the darkness of the final line may be glimpsed the meaning of what lies beyond sight—in shadow, over the horizon, at the bottom of the sea: the mystery, that is, governing the depths of being. Moon is "looking for a bending curve," a scaffold upon which to hang his hopes and fears, and what he finds is a world that "rises horizontally," a seeming oxymoron that proposes a different relationship between subject and object. Gone are the old hierarchies for the poet who from the periphery watches the swaying cosmos watch him. He renounces the romantic enlargement of the self in order to create a horizontal relationship between his own soul and the world—what Chan J. Wu calls a "poetics of humility in which every being breathes with his poetic self. In this sense his poems remind us of our eternal home lost in the desert of modern civilization."

Moon was born in 1970 in Kimcheon, studied Korean literature in college, and works as a producer for the Buddhist Broadcasting System in Seoul. He has published four books of poems, most recently *The Growth of a Shadow*, which furnishes the title for this selection of work from every stage of his career; his honors include the Midang Literary Award, Korea's most prestigious poetry prize, in recognition of the monuments that he raises, in free verse and prose, to all the moments that make up the examined life.

PART I

FLATFISH

In room 302, which houses six patients from Kimcheon Hospital,
she lies in bed with her oxygen mask and struggles with her cancer.
She lies there like a flatfish on the floor of the sea.
I lie down beside her like another flatfish.
When one flatfish glances at another, she bursts into tears.
The emaciated woman cries, with one eye moving into the other.
She looks forward only to death, I look back at the billowing days of her life.
I remember her life in the water, gliding to the right and left,
the lanes she took, the cuckoo's song at noon,
the nights she boiled thin noodles, and the history of her family
which for generations couldn't build mud walls.
I remember the winter day that her legs slowly forked
and her back bent like branches under heavy snow.
The sound of her breath roughens like the bark of an elm.
I know she can no longer see the world beyond death;
one eye has moved darkly into the other.
I swim and twist to the right and left, toward her, I lie down quietly beside her.
She sprinkles on my dry body drops of water drawn through her mask.

JAPANESE DOGWOOD FARMING

The dogwood opens its yellow flowers.
Its shadows are also yellow.
Look, you who complain of your heart's shadow curling up inside you,
trees don't spread their shadows for nothing.
Shadows are also their yearly produce.
The dogwood is farming shadows.
Flowers open in the air, shadows spread on the earth.
The dogwood is farming like a farmer;
its harvest of shadows will weigh about five gallons of yellow millet.

A DOG GIVING HER TEATS TO HER PUPS

A dog is feeding her five pups.
She gives them her teats standing up.
The pups are getting big, it's time for her teats to run dry.
But she feeds them standing up. Perhaps she gives them her dry teats.
It's time to wean her pups of her affection.
Once out of that landscape
no one can enter
it again.

FLOWERS OPEN

When the flowers open
the garden is quiet.

The day is like a sunny wooden veranda.

The naked flesh of the sky
enters the mouths of the flowers
all day long,
moistening the lips of the flowers.

The sky
lays fragrant eggs
in the flowers.

It's wonderful to meet my beloved like this!

AROUND THAT TIME

Dragonflies disappeared from the sky.
My hands were empty.
I kept fingering the day.
I open my eyes again.
My hands are empty.
I pass by a stubborn tombstone.
I am soft, I do not know the word *adamantine*.
The time will come when dragonflies disappear from the sky.
Around that time I too will be free.
Where have they gone,
they who spattered on the leaves?
Did they follow the summer thunder?
Did they follow the summer thunder?

EXTREME POVERTY

Because I got lazy after planting radishes
I missed the roots and stems
and barely harvested the flowers —
white flowers filled with sky.
When people ask me if I grow flowers
in my vegetable garden, I hesitate to answer.
But in the end one butterfly, and then
another, and then a whole flock
comes to rest on the flowers.
Standing on their thin legs
for three or four seconds —
a short time for them —
they fold their wings and sit,
stilling even the wind.
They seem to nap from time to time.
I never had a spot
on which to stand and rest
or a knee to nap on.
My radish garden has become a flower garden,
in the end I'll lose those flowers to the butterflies.

IN THE MOMENT

When the bee slips through, the encased body of the chestnut clacks open.

When water touches the fish, its body bends sharply.

When the needle-sized sunlight speaks, the flower bud bursts into laughter.

When the peak of the mountain magpie pierces the red persimmon, it drops.

I raise a monument to all these moments.

A CICADA ENTERING THE PERSIMMON TREE

A cicada enters the persimmon tree.
It begins to chirp, clinging to the dark-green
persimmon tree. It chirps stiffly, it chirps
from morning until evening, and then it flies away.

We don't know in which part of the heart a cry begins,
nor which sorrow of the tree the cicada descends, chirping.
The tree would also like to lean against the cicada and cry.
Then it closes its mouth and lives for another year.

BOTTOM

You can see the bottom clearly in autumn.
I loved you once but that was in the past.
I sit in a chair and watch
leaves falling in the back yard,
at the foot of the mountain,
falling in a gust of wind.
I close my eyes and listen
to the sound of falling,
leaves brushing against
leaves clinging to the trees,
as when you touch my body
with your body,
as when my breath brushes against
your breath, the sound
of someone taking something
as you received me.
The sound of the earth receiving the falling leaves
is like the sound of a downpour.
The sputtering sound of rain
fills the air.
Once I loved that sound,
which now belongs to the past.
In autumn, even the air reaches the bottom.

A SHORT NAP

When I wake from a nap
I become a tree that shed its blossoms.

Several times a day my soul is left
alone in a strange place.

Today I dreamed of a row deer that kept shying away.

This dream, this daydream becoming ever vaguer,
is like my maudlin sister returning from a visit to our parents.

Rising from a nap, I rinse my mouth with cold water
and clench my fists, I hear the clucking of a mountain pheasant in the bushes.

I stand like a hollow tree in the afternoon.

A BREATH

Let's call the period between the blossoming of a flower
and its falling a breath.
Let's call a breath the period
between a flower letting its body open with a cry
and its opened blossoms crying again
to shed its petals.
Even a flowering tree has lungs like a muddy field;
it breathes with the ebbing tide,
it counts off another when it shakes in the wind.
My father has suffered through sixty winters;
let's call his measly life a breath.

THE GROWTH OF A SHADOW

Dad, don't saw up the persimmon tree.
You cut it down,
because it covered the roof.
So what if it covered the roof?
I can't hold back my tears.
Pneumonia-like clouds hang over the roof,
old cooked rice is on the table at every meal.
We're one body with the growing shadow,
we're sick of the shadow—and we feed on it.
Dad, don't saw up the persimmon tree,
here's wet laughter instead of tears,
shadows unfurling themselves.
I become a shadow, prostrate,
and wind around the night,
recording my sad times.
The borrowed light lingers for a moment in my diary.

NAKED FOOT

A butter clam stretches out its naked foot from the hut of its shell in a fish store.
As the Buddha stretched his feet out of his coffin for his sad disciples, it
  stretches its naked foot.
It's swollen, it soaked too long in the mud and water.
When I touch it, as if to offer my condolences,
it withdraws its foot slowly, as if the touch is its first and last meditation.
Its road, its time, flew by, just like that.
It would go out to meet someone and amble back, just like that;
its foot must always have been naked.
As a bird that lost is mate endures nights with its beak tucked under its wing,
  the clam tucks its naked foot under its wing for the night.
When the shell cries "ah,"
it goes into the street to beg for a meal with its swollen foot.
When it returns to its hut and the stench of poverty,
after wandering all day on its naked foot,
what cried "ah" in the shell must have fed itself,
that cry would have stopped in the dark.

IN MY FATHER'S ABANDONED ORCHARD

Today, my father threw away the fruits of the future.
He cut down plum trees
and apple trees.
Flowers and fruit disappeared
from his field.
Like a mortgage to cover a gambling debt,
two hundred pounds of shadows suddenly vanished,
leaving only a stony field.
The stony field is the intestine of a subarachnoid cyst,
an old breast that cannot be suckled.
My father is the fruit of my subarachnoid cyst.
Today my blind father farms his abandoned orchard
and harvests the stony field, just as he did the year of my birth.
My blind father is my abandoned field.
He made up his mind to will his orchard to me,
he deeded me his abandoned orchard.
He discarded the fruits of the future
which had not ripened and will not rot,
he enters his stony house solitary as the evening.
My old father farms in a strange way,
leaving me a strange inheritance —
how can my inheritance be an abandoned orchard,
the fruits of his labors a stony field?

MIRE

I've kept them in my breast
thinking they were lungs,
and frequented them
as if they were the houses of mourners:
loose sacks in my body,
God's most precious gift,
the swollen breasts that first suckled you,
pupils of eyes that never forget tears,
humble feasts,
the vigor of flowers and the future of fallen leaves,
my body
and my spring
revived by CPR.

PART II

HORIZONTALITY

A dragonfly alights before me,
looks into my eyes with its beady eyes,
spreads its transparent wings horizontally.
Like lotus leaves, it unfurls its linen wings horizontally.
It looks like duckweed floating on water,
it doesn't sway to either side.
But I turn my neck of thoughts right and left,
and see the hole heaved up by a grub on a windy day,
and trace the rough hands of weeds encroaching on the yard.
Even as my thoughts sway and look to my right and left
the dragonfly maintains its tranquil horizontality.
Before this horizontality, the dragonfly lets
the folding screens I raised to my right and left collapse.

WORM POETRY, INC.

A nibbler of white paper, a so-called poet,
I find some happiness growing a little garden.
I visit, worms come,
the garden is our meeting place, our table.
As a joke, after a scholarly meeting, I named
my garden "worm poetry, inc."
The worms and I enjoy sucking
the same breast, we love seamless green holes.
Our only labor is to make these holes with our jaws,
to open up the windpipes of flowers, leaves, sentences.
Strand by pulled strand, the bright green veins of leaves scatter.

YEARNING: INSIDE WATER

There's no other way to say it: the wheel turns.
The squashy wheel seems ready to go anywhere;
it has a knee and a boneless body. Therefore
please hide your teeth when you take pleasure in the sound of water.
I walk inside water;
I open the water and enter the slippery inner flesh
of water and then close the water.
My body becomes wet like a stone
and my ears, eyes, hands, and tongue disappear.
I wish I could live and die like a soft light penetrating water,
and rest in your eyes for a while like shining water scales.
Never have I touched before
this low, softly moving stillness.

WATER LILY

In a small jar I planted a water lily and waited.
As the water froze, it laid down.

Oh, how I love the power of this horizontal plane!

I look carefully and see
a huge wheel turning on the surface of the water.

THE OUTSIDE

A meadow bunting flies
in heavy rain,
quick as a bullet.
Whatever's too quick is sad,
its destination is far away,
its heart yearns for a distant place.
A meadow bunting
swirls and flies
into the rain
that seems to leave no gap at all.
Where will it go
at full speed,
with the power of longing?
Toward home?
A large quiet home like a paulownia leaf?
Or toward the center?
I think it over
but, ah,
I've come to the outside—
too far away.

EXTREME POVERTY (2): A SINGLE ROOM

Entering the Chilsung inn, I knew that after many wanderings I had found a single room.

I watched myself sitting in the room, shedding petals like fatigue. Like a wall in a small room with only a ceiling and a floor, I watched something open and enter and flow out.

Twilight fell on the Kochang bus terminal, Mijin tailor shop, Scale shop, and the Daenong farm machine repair center, and I plodded all the way like a donkey from Shaanxi Sheng.*

One by one the roots, stems, leaves, and flowers of my body are pushed forward and back, in slow-motion video—the guest book of my body, its leaves and stems drying, its roots disappearing. Like Siddhartha, my body is both a palace and a crematorium.

Today I really miss that room, that vegetable.

*A province in northwestern China, which includes portions of the Loess Plateau, the middle reaches of the Yellow River, and the Qinling Mountains.

SACK

Whatever you put in a sack is a sad weight.

There was the head of a household who returned one night with a sack of borrowed rice seed, with snowflakes resembling the snake eyes of spring falling. When I woke at the sound of his footsteps, I was sad, as if the fact that I came from the womb of a concubine had just been revealed; like a field mouse with a pointed mouth, I cried, "Daddy, my body itches, Daddy, my body itches." Thirty years later, the sack still wakes me at dawn and brings to mind the eternity I borrowed from this world.

Spring returned today, and the camellias and white eyes crying for the falling camellias fill a sack. The Milky Way flowing through the intervals of white eyes' songs and the wind swaying at a distance fill a sack. The roof of the wind and my child who dreams a dream of pomegranates fill a sack. And this inseparable thing and I fill a sack.

This morning, carrying a sack of barley malt, of time, I think again of the eternity I borrowed.

FLATFISH (2)

Petals, Flower Decorated Bier

Lastly, I prepared a suit of clothes for her—
the biggest clothes in the world, flowers on a bier.
Though her body is frozen, she wears colorful clothes like petals

She opens the surface of the earth and slowly walks
into the stillness of a jar and lies down like a will.
"Don't cry, my baby. Don't cry."
The flower bier burns into the sky.
No more shadows emerge from her body.

Red Dust Fish

The pallbearers built her grave in the shape of a round-backed fish.
Every grave in the world is a red dust fish,
and she will swim in the waterless sky, she'll go anywhere.

I Took Her Dog Home

A dog leashed in twilight looks like pampas grass in late atumn.
It's molting, its small body grows thinner.
The light is changing in the twilight.
I took the dog she loved to my house through the alley.

WHOOPS!

I have an old duck at home, a female that laid too many eggs,
its behind looks like a brass rice bowl. She lives on anti-depressants,
and one evening a bog stood in her eyes as the plums ripened.
Bog water slid down her face, feathers were pulled out of her flank,
    her flesh was gnawed.
Then a rat crawled toward her from a hole in the earth.
It was greasy. It pretended to speak to her, it drew close to her.
There was the sound of paper being gnawed. A little later, the rat crawled
from the hole with its young swollen like the drowned.
The eyes of two young rats were very clear. They were a family.
The duck, the rats, and I looked at one other. Whoops!

METAPHOR OF A VINE

I'm looking for a bending curve.
From a distance you can see me in it, with a board on my back.

At midday, with a very slow pulse,
I'm looking at the plain surface
of an innocent scaffolding of daylight.
One vine stems from another,
a new bud like poison fired horizontally.
It's like a disease — my addiction to plain surfaces;
it comes from my family history.
I've never built a wall or taken one down.
A world rises horizontally,
like worms crawling on their bellies, furling and unfurling their bodies,
like flattened leeches searching in a rice paddy.
There's a boundary in the mind, when the body rises;
finally the flabby bodies bend from below, one against another.
Later, in my blue burning eyes, the world
will lie horizontally where the wall ends
and die by the coiling of its neck.

THE FAVORITE AROMA OF COOKED RICE

My appetite is completely gone.
Without thinking, I scooped the strange aroma of cooked rice into my
  bowl of thoughts.
I came across that refreshing aroma of rice circling the kitchen in Dasol Temple.
When Manhae* and Dongli** took to the cold wooden floor at dawn,
their spirits refreshed like a hanji***at the sound of snowflakes
  falling on frozen leaves,
they must have satisfied their hunger with a bowl of this aroma.
The aroma of cooked rice, rinsing everything else away,
was laid on my thinking like a hat after my visit to Dasol Temple.
Ah, I'd like to crouch on it long enough to cultivate my spirit.
The aroma lingers on me this morning!
Which is why I completely lost my appetite for regular food.

*Pen name of Yongun Han, a Korean poet and Buddhist monk. He published
  his only book of poems, *Silence of the Beloved*, in 1925.
**A famous Korean novelist whose books include *The Cross of Saban* (1955)
  and *Shaman* (1939).
*** Traditional Korean paper made from the mulberry tree.

A STRANGE VASE

The wandering Buddha didn't stay long under the tree.
Where should you wander to let your mind rest?
I feel sad to be fated to return to a place.
I have a premonition that my rot will begin slowly in some place like a pond.
Today I'm staring at a flower vase;
like fish caught in a net, the flowers caged in the vase
make it look as if the water is filled with the dried scales of dead fish.
Their fins sank, their eyes have no spirit, like the walls.
The faces of the flowers darkened, like charcoal drawings.
The vase has the knack of making fresh flowers wilt in a day.
It can even show me wilting in the very spot where I stand.

METAPHOR OF THE DAY MOON

The place where my life began to crumble.

A squishy package from a distant place,
a thin rice paper door and loose fence,
a wooden floor with a bowl of cold water.
Flowers, birds, even people
hold it like water, then let it go.
The cooling furnace brightens for a moment.

A word of farewell flowing clearly in my ear.
A word pouring out like chuff from a sack to become white light.

GINKGO TREE BEHIND UNMOON TEMPLE

In the yard behind Unmoon Temple stood a thousand-year-old ginkgo tree.
Yellow leaves piled up on the spot where its shadow used to fall.
Leaves were slowly falling and piling up on the tedious shadow of its body.
There was no movement at all
except the tree shedding its own leaves.
Falling should always be like this. It was so beautiful—
the tree looked like a golden temple, with a golden pond at its base.
The golden scales of carp were falling into the water and piling up on the bottom.
I wish my last breath would slip away like that, when I die.
I wish I could unload everything from my body, to be free of the wind
    and clean after death.
I wish I could close my eyes first and hear the sound of my body collapsing
    when I die.

SURPRISED BY COLOR

A vine crawls around
a dead tree
up to the top branch.
Under the limb:
a small pond.
Under the water light:
Chinese minnows
trail shadows
swollen like soaked rice
with their naked feet,
and feel
the green forehead
of slimy stones.
They're quite indifferent.
They're calm, at leisure.
Startled in the middle of their leisure,
their shadows run away.
A small leaf
has fallen
on the water:
it has an autumnal color.

PART III

THE DELIVERY OF A JAPANESE APRICOT TREE

An aging Japanese apricot tree brightens
once its flowers open like a navel.
It's like the delivery of a stubborn old woman;
the womb of the tree is old and withered,
but the juice pouring from its deep valley grows flowers,
which smell like the flesh of a newborn.
The tree sits absentmindedly with its swollen breasts.

CONFUSION

While I stood in the backyard one autumn night
an insect cried.
Wind blew,
sweeping away the mountain bamboo leaves.
The sounds of the insect
and the bamboo leaves
took turns.
Once
their sounds
overlapped;
but the sound of the bamboo leaves didn't drown out the insect,
which didn't sit on the leaves
or anything like that.
It struck me
that I really misunderstood
the word *confusion.*
With that word
I showed off
too much.

ALLUDING TO A TOAD: POETRY

Because your face stirred me where my step stopped,
I looked around your house and yard slowly,
very slowly, before I left.

My poor life, my poetry,
will be dedicated to this damp place.

FOR NO REASON

I passed the stone wall
A cricket was chirping in the wall.
They say a huge serpent used to live there.
One stone wall after another.
The cricket followed me, chirping.
I hurried home
and laid my head on a wooden pillow.
I lay motionless in the empty room
but the cricket followed me,
chirping in the wooden pillow.
When the room grew dark
and night fell into night,
tears fell drop by drop
for no reason.

FLOWER POT

I thought about
the love farm

and discovered that I'm a lover who betrays himself.

My labor and I
watered the dying flower pot

but the time of snow melting on the distant mountain
flew by.

I watered the dying flower pot,

grass returned
from somewhere
to the spot where it withered,

grass returned to sprout;
its body grew big
and opened flowers
to finally become a woman.

Melancholy, swaying in the wind,
she stood behind me with tears in her eyes
when I sat with my back turned.

I never asked her
where she came from,
just as nobody asked me.

With this flower pot
we excelled, we walked ahead
or slowed down and walked behind

With this flower pot
we were lovers passing like cloud shadows.
I'm a lover who betrays himself.

Therefore, my love,
please draw water
to fill the folds
and quench our thirst
when we meet each other.

ME, A WHEELBARROW

There lies a wheelbarrow
in which my old father hauls manure to the vineyard.
Sometimes it rests all day without working,
and today is that day.
With nothing to do,
I go around pushing the cart.
It flies like a ship or a fish;
the wheel rolls into
the bamboo grove and the cave,
but doesn't go too far.
When it grows dark I stop
and come back empty.
I put it down gently where it was before.
I don't know who pushed this wheelbarrow,
and me, for no reason at all.

ONE'S WHOLE LIFE

The evening deepens
and I see puppies seeking their mother's teats.
Like the evening, she lies on her back on the wet ground,
and five puppies whose eyes have not fully opened
push their heads against one other
to find their evening meal.
They will not live in other places,
this is their whole life.

MAGNOLIA

I'd like to be a worker in a field in spring.

My mother, who peddles bush-clover baskets, brings hot meals

today to the rice paddy, her toenails have never been free of dirt.

IT SWAYS

I look at the cosmos:
I'm the center
and the cosmos is the periphery.
Wind blows and the cosmos
sways, I look at
the swaying cosmos.
When I think the cosmos sways,
the center sways.
As water drains from the bathtub,
so the center
moves from me to the cosmos
gradually.
I'm the periphery
and the cosmos is the center.
I sway and look at the cosmos,
the cosmos sways
and looks at me.

LOVE

Like a carpenter bee hovering around the pumpkin flowers,

like a suckling baby drowsing on his mother's nipple,

it wishes to live in the smell of that plump flesh.

SPRING SUNLIGHT

No trouble today
even for the fool who hid a stolen handful of it in a vase, and fell asleep.

All day I'm full, I'm not hungry at all.

I stroke myself for the first time.

Today man is also a plant raised by the sky.

EXTREME POVERTY (3): THE FIELD

I came to the empty field.

Holding a rice bowl with its ears chipped off,

I begged for light.

I dried my clothes as I used to dry my hair tails.

If I lie naked,

the hours of half a day, like the shed skin of a cicada, last for ten months.

Like an embryo in the belly, my ears and eyes open anew.

I will lend the field to you who promised to come along with me.

DISTANCE

Like the spot where the grass snake drags its belly, flattening the grass,
like the depth of the night in which the goose returns to its pen, calling and calling,
like the spot where I stood before I walked after the goose and then looked back,
like the mountain trail on which a coffin was carried in a blizzard a season ago,
like the flabby calves of my uncle dead for three days, like the downpour long ago,
the distance that nobody talked to me about.

A JOCULAR POSTMAN

The mailman is busy all day;
he doesn't stop
by the cucumber flowers,
to my dismay
he pedals down the lane on his bicycle,
still holding letters with their hidden sentences.
He turns his head toward me
and whistles:
"Someday you'll get a letter."
He clasps his hands
provocatively,
he dons his summer skirt,
his butterfly clothes.

WRINKLED SHIRT

A shirt hanging on the wall,
its sleeve and armpit wrinkled.
Wind and cloud squeeze into the shirt,
which wears an ugly frown.
Even a small titmouse flies away from it.
The arm that took off the shirt
will ache even after a night's sleep.
You should have pulled, pushed, lifted,
and put things down, you who resemble things.
A shirt hanging askew on the wall, its outline
crumpled like an old paper bag used for medicine.
Something must have been inside it.
More wrinkles should have been inside it.

PART IV

POND AT DAWN

As hot water circles the blue tears of the tea leaves,
as a vacant room in a cheap inn receives the wandering guest—

a quiet, secluded pond
and a wild duck about to soar.

LIKE A SLEEPING DOG

Like a sleeping dog with his belly and chin on the ground
I pass the noon hour of this world.
My dream crawls casually along the bottom of the sunlight.
Without knowing my neck is chained,
I pass the noon hour with my slack chain.
There's nothing special I want.
I see crepe-myrtle blooming in my eyes.
I close my eyes like a worm, like a dog lying down.
I pass the noon hour of this world
before the bottom of the world cools,
before my dream goes cold.

LOVE OF A WALNUT TREE

When I returned to the walnut tree, my heart sank at the sight of it standing like a woman with her womb removed.

A late flock of cicadas clung to its branches, sucking it dry.

All summer I heard the crying of the tree
without entering its core, my ears are so gullible.

When I returned to the walnut tree, my heart twisted like fire dust, and I guessed that my confession, like the wind, would not be forgiven either.

FIRST LOVE

The woman with eyes as white as the new moon.
I can't see her over my jutting cheekbone.
The woman in the vanishing well,
the woman who made me hot,
as if she was fired stone.
But my mind cannot find her,
trapped like a diving beetle among water plants;
only the singing of the black swallow makes a house call
to my mind, dry as a garlic clove.
Like a jar stand facing away, toward the backyard,
my lonely love cries in the empty jar.

ANT

You could imagine that a black ant crawled then stopped, lost in thought.

Mrs. Bongsan bent over to wash her breasts,
and her nipples dried like frosted lotus persimmon at the end of the season.
She stroked the barley on the terrace stone at harvest time, her mouth wild
  as barley seed.
She used to come home black as charcoal after drinking at a party after dark.
She raised me on the other side of the wall.
Mrs. Bongsan, stooping, looking a little risky.

DRIZZLE

On a day like this
I might meet
a stutterer who utters words as if to touch a bough of sumac.
The interval is full of risk.
This thin rain falls,
and I look for something to return.
Salvia,
with its thin red waist.

THE EMPTY HOUSE

It's like the place you left to follow the muddy road. With nowhere to rest my mind, it's like old shoes left out in the wind and rain. I crouch by the firebox to rekindle the ember, but the flues are broken.

The wind raises its fingers and tears a hole in the paper window. The house of memory built with straws that we carried in our beaks collapses in the wind. If you return long after, and see the jars standing side by side, and find my molded longings in them, you better sweep the yard clean with the worn bush-clover broom.

MY MIND IN THE HAUNTED HOUSE

My mind, which couldn't even follow the gravelly road, is in the haunted house.

How difficult it is to hear the sound of the wheel again!
The bicycle stands by the dusty farm tools.

My old love is gone, and I sit alone in the haunted house, like a yellow-spotted serpent.
The wind sits on the saddle, slowly turning the wheel.

How foolish it is to oil the rusted props!
How useless to fill the air and wait!

PASSING THE CAVE

It was always difficult to drive the cow through the cave. Even animals with red lights in their eyes hesitate in the dark.

We pass through the cave, scraping the wall with a stick. The cave is a huge jar of darkness! And just as the sound is amplified when I push my head into the jar and shout, it hurts that sometimes the sound is not my own.

Like the cow in my youth, when I bruised my knees splashing in the water in the cave, the road never opens to people unprepared for love. Only when you can forgive, let your mind stray, will you pass through the cave intact. Only then will this long darkness end.

OH, MOTHER

I saw a herd of black goats raising their horns. They stood firm, their beards flying in the north wind like raised bamboo spears, and nursed their kids. They kicked up dust with their hind legs, they spread themselves in a row in the field.

SEDUCTION

The old barefoot man carrying thorns on his back seduces me.
That bunch of thorns seduces me,
moving bones which could be excavated from a weed-covered grave.
The old man looks at me with the eyes of a cow's tongue and licks my body.
The bush of thorns ties me up.
Those stout bare feet lying in the road carry my life.

HACKBERRY FAMILY

The house on the small hill opened in every direction.
Birds scattered during the day, flew back to the hackberry,
settled one by one facing the same way.
Those that gaze together are sad and frightened.
As in a family with a poor father,
a young one with chapped cheeks was in the flock.
When it grew dark, the tree took its family and disappeared.

RED CAMELLIA

Seolyo, the Buddhist nun of Silla, is said to have returned to secular life because
    she was enchanted by spring flowers.

On spring days, I'd like to be a blind fish weeping in the garden of a small temple.

Even without the thunderous crack of the thawing pond,

I'd like to weep quietly in my confinement, on spring nights.

Though I live as a heartless cook in a temple, serving food to a man from far away,

I'd like to be a cheek red as camellias in the temple yard,

for love lifts its veil slightly on spring days.

MILLSTONE

It looks like the anklebone of my farmer uncle casually stretched out on the wooden floor.

It looks like the old hackberry, on the outskirts of the village, with layers of wrinkles on its trunk.

It looks like a sad stone tower that the dead stones built themselves.

It looks like our pregnant goat during its autumn molt.

It looks like what made the man who lost his love shed tears like mung bean flowers.

My grandmother, turning that millstone, doesn't seem to suffer anymore.

THE SPOT WHERE THE FLOWERS WERE

To think about it is to sit on the vacant seat,
to sit on the empty spot where the flower petals were.

To miss it is to sit on the vacant seat,
to sit like red petals and keep it empty, against your will.

WILD PEAR TREE

A pear tree stood in front of Baekdam Temple.

Its fruits, small as grains of rice, hung from the tree.

Suntanned, rinsed by the wind, they shrank.

The tree must have watched the fruits it grew with its own body wither.

I wonder if anyone ever watched me with such a loving gaze.

A sad face wavered on the wild pear tree and passed on.

STATION-FACING BARBERSHOP

It makes me happy that my afternoons sometimes end in the barbershop.

Part of the signboard is erased; only "Station-facing barbershop" remains.
The station is long gone. The barber insists on keeping the name.

When I visit, I recall the landscape of my mother scraping out the inside of a gourd.
The hunchback barber scrapes my scalp with his hard dry hand,
and we giggle together, stealing glimpses at the obscene picture on the wall.

The world's basest twilight lives in the barbershop—
a wilting flower releasing its fragrance in the air.

Though he lives above running water, like a water plant,
the hunchback barber cleans my water steeped in waste.

TONGUE

Wakened at dawn,
I think in desperation
of my sick mother.

If a bit of straw got into my eye
when I was young,
you rinsed your mouth with cold water
and licked
my eyeball,
my soul
with your tongue,
the softest flesh.
.

Even when you dozed off
by the firebox,
fire passed from the *ondol*
to the chimney
in your eyes.

On the 7th of July, on the lunar calendar,
you prayed to the stone Buddha,
rubbing your hands in devotion:
now that Buddha is sitting
in your eyes.
.

I wonder in what life
will I receive life
from someone other than you
and become a cruel bamboo comb.

In what life
will my tongue sweep away
those stone-like
eyeballs?

I crane my neck
and weep
until the morning's wet.

ONE DAY, WHAT WE BELIEVED TO BE THE CENTER

Like water that carries the mountain shadow into the rice paddy,
there comes a day when I miss a man.

One afternoon, when new buds shoot from the trees like the eyes of a crab,
I gaze at the red magnolias in ecstasy.

What we believed to be the center may not be the center at all;
as those tiny tender buds are the center of the tree
it occurs to me that what is condensed, globule-like, is not the center.

My longing may not be for just one person.
Old faces equal to the color of water
may drive me to tears
one afternoon, when I look at flowers.

As all the centers of darkness are equal when I walk alone on an unpaved road,
     on the last night of a lunar month,
a single drop of water cannot take the mountain shadow into the rice paddy.

A WOMAN CALLED THE LAST DAY OF THE MONTH

Though she was black as lacquer and cold as ice,
and ants had dug tunnels in her face,
and her legs were thinner than a deer's,
there were many days I entered the spacious yard of her mind
and let my mind rest.
I called that strange peace the sad last day of the month.
I last saw my grandmother when I was fifteen.

LOVERS

The wind was coming over.
India ink was spreading on the dry ink stone.
Many winds were coming over.
They came in a group.
Lotus leaves bustled about the field.
So beautiful,
the gentle eyes of the lotuses that recognize one man among so many winds,
the round sound spreading through the air
in search of Sahasrabhuja.*

*A thousand-armed bodhisattva who embodies the compassion of every Buddha.

ABOUT THE POET

Taejoon Moon was born in Kimcheon in 1970 and studied Korean Literature at college. He has published four volumes of poems: *Murmuring Backyard* (2000), *Naked Foot* (2004), *Flatfish* (2006), and *The Growth of a Shadow* (2008). Moon has received the East and West Literary Award, the Nojak Literary Award, the Yoosim Literary Award, the Soweol Literary Award, and the Midang Literary Award, Korea's most prestigious poetry prize.

ABOUT THE TRANSLATORS

Won-Chung Kim, professor of English at Sungkyunkwan University in Seoul, has translated eight books of Korean poems into English, including Chiha Kim's *Heart's Agony*. He has also translated John Muir's *My First Summer in the Sierra* into Korean.

Christopher Merrill's books include *Brilliant Water* (poetry), *Things of the Hidden God: Journey to the Holy Mountain* (nonfiction), and many translations. He directs the University of Iowa's International Writing Program.